"Hear" I Am!!

"Hear" I Am!!

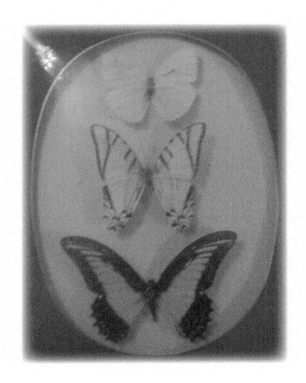

Jennifer Beilis

To order additional copies of this book, contact:
Xlibris LLC
1-888-795-4274
www.Xlibris.com
Orders@Xlibris.com
552179

"Hear" I am!! is a personal story with universal application.

Jennifer Beilis's story is a powerful one; she and her family endure many health and life challenges, but through it all she maintains a desire to learn and reflect. Anyone who has hearing loss, or any sort of health challenge can benefit from reading this book. Mark Rosal, President, Ear Gear

Information about the Author

I wish everyone the best of luck, health and hope that my autobiography motivates people to believe in themselves and to achieve their individual goals in a positive manner. I have questions in certain areas of the book for you to reflect upon your life to learn and grow as a person. My book will help parents, teachers, educators, and employers to learn how to help individuals with disabilities. This book's goal is to help individuals realize that people who have a disability can go to college and work as well as anyone else with the proper accommodations in place. In addition my book can also teach you how to make changes in your life by realizing your inner strength!

I am very grateful for my education in the following schools: Brookdale Community College that is located in Lincroft, NJ, where I earned my Associate's Degree in Social Sciences. They currently offer Associate's, Bachelor's and Master's degrees being partnered with other schools. Then I graduated from Rowan University, that is located in Glassboro, New Jersey, where I earned my Bachelor's degree in Psychology and also am in Alpha Phi Omega, National Coed Service Fraternity. Rowan University has Bachelor's and Master's degree programs. Lastly, I graduated from New York University, located in New York and earned my Master's degree in Education and Deafness Rehabilitation as well as my (SCPI) Sign Language Proficiency Interview. They offer Bachelor's, Master's and PHD degrees at New York University. I had excellent support from most of my professors.

My book is dedicated to my grandparents, my father, my family and to CG (who you will see was my mentor throughout my hearing loss) as well as many hearing loss affiliations or associations (HLAA Hearing Loss Association of America a national support group for those with any level of hearing loss, (ALDA) Association of Late Deafness that helps people with all hearing loss levels. There are other companies that helped me as well such as: Sea–Band (products that help with Meniere's and other items, Ear for Gears (helps with wind, moisture and prolongs the life of the hearing aids, Dry and Store (sanitizes the hearing aids, Nature's Nutrition, (Peter Marino, pharmacist and health food store owner), Canine Companions (provided a picture and permission to help the reader learn about their services they are an organization that trains dogs for people with disabilities) and Shamrock Boutique (hair and nail salon.). Alpha Phi Omega (APO) is a national coed Service Fraternity that taught me many skills of advocacy that enabled me to transfer to the work force and communicating with others. Thank you for your support and believing in me to become a strong advocate for hearing loss and other disabilities which has taught me inner discipline to be the best person I can be.

Note to the reader: "This story is meant to be uplifting to the reader. I am now having a stronger and more positive outlook and wonderful support system. Illness is always a difficult thing and affects the whole family. However; you will not lose your sense of being and the power of believing that you can feel better in life. There is always hope to get better from the situations we are in. I also use a time and reflection and write things out that I want to track every so often be it my finances, my life or how I had handled something before and how would I handle it again? Have you ever tried to journalize or use free association? Free association is writing about a topic or a word not worrying about sentence format or spelling. Writing has always been an outlet for me to get my thoughts together and making a plan of action for situations in my life. Also, exercising, meditating or other hobbies can be an outlet as well."

I was diagnosed with hearing loss when I was five years old. When I grew up in New York, I wore one hearing aid and I always remembered how children can be cruel because someone is "different from the norm." I felt that my family did not understand my hearing loss and would scream "Jen it's time for dinner." and I would never answer as the door was closed when I was studying. This caused many communications problems growing up. Also, my dad and brother always talked in a low monotone voice that everyone struggled to hear them. My brother and I selected a female Shetland Sheepdog that we named Patches; She had a patch on her forehead. She loved to alert me to the phone or doorbell ringing by barking. My grandparents had moved to New Jersey and we followed shortly after. They had selected Princess, a beautiful Sheltie, who was almost as big as a Collie (think Lassie), who had a beautiful disposition. I wondered how can I could help myself so I could understand the hearing loss and help others?

In the sixth grade we moved to New Jersey, and I found the tormentors of the teachers and students to be very demeaning. After being relentlessly picked on, I chose not to wear hearing aids from the seventh grade to community college. I always had a terrific GPA. I was able to hear well enough not to use the hearing aids in the classroom throughout those years as it was milder. However; when I went to Brookdale Community College, the material was much more challenging and I struggled to hear the professors. My family had improved slightly by using the intercom system in our house that we had to call me for dinner instead of screaming and getting angry at me for no reason at all. My parents always instilled the emphasis of higher education, morals and values in me to help me best the person I could be. Reflecting back on my family I have a younger brother and two parents. My dad passed away recently to leukemia and we miss him dearly, as well as the loss of my grandparents due to cancer. I was always close to my immediate family who were there for my special moments in life.

There are two types of hearing losses: They are conductive and sensioneural or nerve loss. Conductive hearing loss: can be reversed it occurs when sound waves are blocked from reaching nerves that allow one to hear. (Everyday Health Media.com). Sensioneural or nerve loss can be caused by "fluid building up in the eardrum. It can be caused from an infection, tumor or fevers. Sometimes surgery can be performed on "perforated eardrums, narrowing of the ear canal and tumors of the middle canal, otosclerosis which is a stiffening of bones that conduct sound from one ear drum to the inner ear" (Everyday Health Media. com.) Nerve loss can also be helped by someone who has lost their hearing can use a Cochlear Implant that has three parts, headpiece processor and receiver. This is surgically performed and you have to remap the brain to hear again. (Everyday Health Media.) I was diagnosed with a Sensioneural hearing loss with unknown causes.

Reflection: What experiences did you have in your life that was a challenge to you from your childhood to adulthood years? What did you learn from it and how does it affect you today?

Brookdale Administration Center

03/16/2014 16:37

BANKIER
LIBRARY

ehhange

03/16/2014 16:40

03/16/2014 16:34

03/16/2014 16:41

When I attended Brookdale Community College I will never forget a friend in college. He stated: "If you choose to hear then you will function better in school or work." At the time, I had just lost my grandfather to cancer (this was my first real life altering event) and that taught me more self-awareness to use creative writing to express my feelings. Princess died shortly after grandpa and we always made sure to keep our grandma's spirits up by actively engaging her in our plans to shop or plan family get together. I went to a hearing aid dispenser and was fitted with two analog (non-digital or basic) hearing aids. This helped me to hear in the classroom. Special Services is required to assist any students who have various special needs and provide services at no additional cost. In retrospect, I had started to learn how to advocate for myself to ask a professor if I can sit in the front of the classroom, tape the lectures, and have time and a half on tests or to repeat something they or a student stated. You will need to have a disability that is documented and approved by the college to obtain the accommodations. It is always advised to ask for accommodations that match the disability and in a polite manner. I also was active in the Special Services department and had organized an event for the college and public to learn what disabilities people had and that you can be a success in college. I felt it was a great experience for all involved. I earned my Associate's Degree in Social Sciences from Brookdale Community College and felt that I had wonderful teachers who helped me by allowing me to sit in the front of the room and taped the lectures.

Rowan University

After I transferred to Rowan University, I faced new challenges such as: being on my own for the first time, and I needed accommodations in the dorm for a loud phone ringer. Some of the professors were helpful. I had used closed captioning at home (this provided the words on the television for the deaf or hard of hearing) for many years. However; the VHS tapes did not have closed captioning on them at the time. I thought it was ludicrous to drive a hundred miles to listen to the tapes at home. I contacted the school's newspaper and submitted an article about this situation. Finally, a high school across the street allowed me to use their equipment.

I was very rebellious about wearing my hearing aids in college and especially in front of my family and in public. I felt that I was different from everyone else. Some of the teachers were helpful with my hearing loss by allowing me to have the following accommodations: taping the class, sitting in the front, and a quiet place to take the exams.

Alpha Phi Omega

NATIONAL SERVICE FRATERNITY

However; in my last year of college, I pledged APO, Alpha Phi Omega. "Alpha Phi Omega is a national coeducational service fraternity—college students gathered together in an organization based on fraternalism and founded on the principles of the Boy Scouts of America. Its purpose is to develop leadership, promote friendship and provide service to humanity. Since 1925, more than 415,000 students have chosen Alpha Phi Omega, making the Fraternity the nation's largest Greek letter fraternity." We were always required to have homework time and pass our classes to stay in the organization. In addition, we had to hold several events for the fraternity. I held a seminar on hearing loss in college (with the help of a psychologist on campus) to educate others which helped me to learn to advocate more for myself. I finally met another person who had hearing loss who tried to motivate me. In addition, to this I performed a service for the college to have awareness for World AID'S Day by having students get tested and raffle off condoms. I was able to raise money for the fraternity that an organization matched as well. I also held a seminar by myself and another fraternity to promote AIDS awareness by having a raffle and a psychologist to help me with the event to teach the community to practice abstinence or safe sex. I invited three individuals who had AIDS give lectures to the college to prove that young people can contract the illness and it taught many students to practice safe intercourse. I will never forget a mother yelling "Why are you doing this?" I wanted to prevent teenage or college age pregnancies and sexually transmitted diseases such as AIDS. All it takes is one person to have a belief to change the world or someone's thinking and I am very proud to make a difference in the world! I earned my Bachelor's degree in Psychology in 1996 from Rowan University. I was and still am very proud of all my accomplishments at Rowan University where I learned to be a leader, organizer and an advocate. We were able to give Patches five more years to live after I found a tumor, but she died in 1997.

After graduation I returned to the workforce and to obtain my Master's Degree in Counseling; that did not work out. I had a major head on car accident in 1997 and had to learn to walk and function. Looking back after the three months I began to regain my strength I had developed problems with my balance, inner ear, back and neck injuries. After returning to the retail store, I quit the Master's program and moved back home for a few years to earn money to buy a car. I had to tell the boss and other coworkers that I was hard of hearing in order for me to function on the job. I found that hiding the hearing loss on the job was not to my advantage.

In turn, I went to work once again in retail. I was still ashamed and hid my hearing loss at work. People started to question my intelligence level and gave me strange looks. I decided to talk to the manager and tell the store about my hearing loss. She wrote down the tasks for me to make it much easier for me to understand than struggling to hear her.

Reflection: Did you have struggles in the workforce or college because of an illness? What did you do about it? Did you change your situation that you were or are in currently? Did you advocate for yourself or allow it to fester inside you? How would you handle the situation next time?

I started to build self-confidence. I was learning to ask people to please repeat or reword what they said. I had to constantly remind my bosses and co-workers that I had a hearing loss. This was the start of a valuable lesson.

Reflection: I would ask myself how can I help myself truly understand my hearing loss so I could advocate for myself and others? Would this be an easy or a hard path for me? Have you been in a situation that you wanted to change in your life? Were you so frustrated or overwhelmed that you could not achieve your goals?

I had dated many people in college and did not meet "Mr. Right." There were some marriage proposals along the way which I declined. I was always searching for that special person in my life to share a very deep love, values, honesty and communication. My parents taught me that a marriage always needs to have a strong foundation.

A series of life altering moments began when I wanted to learn to accept my hearing loss as a part of me and not to be rebellious and shy about this. One day, my father, cut an article in the paper about hearing loss written by CG (permission to call her that as my mentor throughout my hearing loss.) I had contacted her through email for almost two years before meeting in real life. I had attended a hearing loss function in New Jersey and it was my first experience observing sign language. My eyes started to "open up" as I was inspired to further my education and dreamed of accepting my hearing loss. I still wondered if I would meet Mr. Right. I was working full time in a retail position and had asked one of my friends who lived in Pennsylvania to go online and find husbands for us. Little did we know, she was successful in doing this for both of us! Marc had called me while I was still living with my family and we spoke for three hours on the phone. I knew right away he was the one for me by his affectionate ways, kind and gentleness. We agreed to meet three days later to go on a date. It is so funny looking back in time; I peeked through the window and there he was tall, handsome with dark features and grew up in Brooklyn, New York and the same religion. During the date I could tell how kind of a person he was by letting the senior citizens go first in the parking lot, opening the door for me and treating me with respect. I could tell "I was hit by a thunderbolt" by his kiss and knew right away he was the one for me! We had a very nice courtship that had begun! We were growing closer every day, yet I still had more growing and learning about myself to conquer. While I was working at a retail store, our courtship started to blossom. This was the first time that I decided to inform the managers about my hearing loss and had them write down the instructions for me so it would be easier to hear them. I trained people for the cashier position and worked in ladies sportswear.

HLAA (Hearing Loss Association of America) had a convention on hearing loss in New Orleans; which my parents helped finance. Marc was my boyfriend then, now we are married over thirteen years. I thought we were going to get engaged at this point but we did later on. I was glad to find out that his father had hearing loss so that Marc was able to understand my struggles. I was very active in HLAA as well to help other people with hearing loss by promoting awareness in meetings. I helped to pass different laws to have babies hearing tested at birth. Early detection is crucial to helping the baby hear correctly from as early as possible. I also helped to advocate laws to have signs put in the hospitals as well if you need to have interpreter and some places even have beepers to alert the patient their name is being called.

Before arriving in New Orleans we had to wait five hours for delays because of thunderstorms. One lady who was deaf asked us to let her know when the phone was ringing so she could talk on the phone. There are many levels of hearing loss: hard of hearing, deaf (those who lost their hearing later in life) and Deaf when someone uses American Sign Language to communicate. We realized there was no Closed Captioning or CART (a sign to show you what is being said out loud used in meetings or shows etc. for the Deaf or Hard of Hearing.) The airline did compensate us with two discounts for future use after pointing this out that there were no accommodations being made for the people on the plane to know what was going on with the delays.

When we finally arrived and entered the hotel I was amazed by the people at the HLAA convention. This was my first experience with hearing guide dogs that are trained for the deaf, hard of hearing, blind or other disabilities. There are other devices such as: flashing lights (alert system to tell someone if there is a person at the door, alarm clocks, emergencies in public places, and FM systems (which is a device that brings the speakers voice closer to the person who is wearing hearing aids to help them with fatigue, assists people who are hard of hearing in a meeting, school, medical or work situation. Many people with hearing loss are extremely fatigued from trying to listen all day what is going on in their day and this device helps in meetings, work, school, or a one on one conversation as well and American Sign Language. My sense of awareness of many forms of hearing loss, peaked at this time. I learned that hearing loss ranged from mild to Deaf and there were different cultures to learn about each one! Little did I know at the time how different they were! Where did I belong in the hearing or deaf world? I struggled to hear and felt it was hard to fit in with the hearing population as well as the Deaf world. In the hearing world, many people did not care to repeat themselves. In the Deaf World, they communicated in American Sign Language which I did not know as of yet.

CG was the HLAA President and Co-Founder of the New Jersey chapter at the time. I was so overwhelmed to finally "meet in person" I knew we would become instant lifelong friends. CG dedicated her life to advocate for hearing loss. There were many lectures that we attended on hearing loss that helped people to learn how to be assertive about their hearing loss, drums/music—a form of music therapy for relaxation as well as a 1950's gathering etc. They have chapter meetings in each state as well as national conventions yearly to teach people about hearing loss. Rocky Stone was the founder for HLAA, who was Deaf and losing his sight. He was later able to have a Cochlear Implant (a device for the Deaf to be able to hear thru surgery that has to learn to map the brain.) I was fortunate enough to meet him and felt honored that he founded the wonderful organization.

One of the most important days of my life was at the HLAA convention when I stood up in front of thousands of people and asked "Who would want to pay for my Master's Degree or hire me? (I had my AA in Social Sciences and Bachelor's Degree in Psychology). I had three different colleges tell me about programs to learn about hearing loss. I was awarded many scholarships due to my helping with advocating for Hearing Loss Association of America and other agencies. I chose to attend New York University's Master's Degree, Education and Deafness Rehabilitation as it was much closer to home and I was falling in love with Marc as well. I became active in HLAA to learn more about coping with hearing loss and a professional standpoint. I learned to have the speaker reiterate or write down what they were saying to help me hear them. This helped me communicate more effectively. I thought that Marc was going to propose in New Orleans when he stated that he had a surprise for me.

When attending a meeting for hearing loss, Marc and I performed a skit of a hearing individual and a hard of hearing individual. We showed the public the incorrect way to present oneself by screaming "Jen time for dinner," when I was in another room with the door closed. The correct way would be for the hearing spouse to open the door, tap me on the shoulder and say nicely "please join me for dinner." In other words, you must have the person's attention first and then talk about what you may need.

I was introduced to ALDA (Association of Late Deafened Adults (d), which is an organization for all levels of hearing loss. I was awarded a scholarship for my advocacy in the field. In the past, I was their secretary. They welcome everyone and have conventions as well. They provide people with information about hearing loss and also offer a scholarship for students to finish their education.

Many of the people (d) have lost their hearing later in life, but still may have normal speech as they grew up with normal hearing. This could have happened from various medical problems. Some will obtain a Cochlear Implant or learn American Sign Language, but for the most part will identify with the hearing culture.

Photo credit to: Chris Nichols

In my Master's Degree program at New York University, the program consisted of students and staff with all levels of hearing losses that ranged from hearing to hard of hearing, and finally culturally Deaf. The dean was always very supportive of my goals. You were required to pass the SCPI (Sign Language Proficiency Interview) in NY to obtain your degree. That test was videotaped and reviewed to prove that you had the skill level required to pass the test.

My thesis was about accepting my hearing loss in terms of knowledge and insight about hearing dogs, assistive devices and support groups. We learned primarily about hearing loss but also did learn about other disabilities as well and how to advocate for those who have a disability. I felt that my training helped me to flourish and develop a greater sense of self-worth in myself and in my marriage.

03/16/2014 21:16

Marc had proposed to me in 1999 a little over a year that we were dating and he asked my parents as well (we are both old fashioned) and married in the year 2000! We could not wait to start our new lives together. We had a beautiful millennium wedding with our wonderful families and friends. I will never forget how hard my parents and grandma looked at the various vendors from the florist, band, invitations and bridal showers to help us. I was working full time and attending graduate school and taking American Sign Language classes at Brookdale Community College. We were only engaged for nine months before getting married. We had a beautiful wedding with a professional band, lilies and engraved invitations. My aunt, my mom's sister, encouraged the wedding guests to sing "Happy Birthday" to her and had a real flower cake. We have a family tradition that my parents were married the day before my grandma's birthday and we followed that tradition! We had an unforgettable honeymoon in Orlando, Florida. We moved into a one bedroom apartment and lived there for nine months to start our lives together.

I had performed two internships in graduate school in New York and New Jersey. I learned that there is vocational rehabilitation in each state that may help with services such as paying for school, a job coach, hearing aids or assistive devices. There are certain accommodations that are available to someone with a hearing loss such as: hearing aids, sitting in the front of the room, using an FM device (brings sound closer to you), an interpreter either for American Sign Language or lip-reading) a quiet place to take a test and time and half if needed. Also, adequate lighting is a must so the person with hearing loss can lip-read the speaker. In the Deaf culture, an individual will require an interpreter for the classroom or public places. I was introduced to the Division of Deaf and Hard of Hearing as well as the Monthly Communicator. They advertise all New Jersey events that are related to hearing loss articles, services, social gathering, new technology and employment in the field.

Director's Corner

By David Alexander, *Ph.D., Director, Division of the Deaf and Hard of Hearing (DDHH)*

Communication access and services resulting in employment is a topic of utmost importance to people who are Deaf and hard of hearing. This past January 2014, Alice Hunnicutt, Director of the Division of Vocational Rehabilitative Services (DVRS), was a guest presenter to the DDHH Advisory Council meeting. Ms. Hunnicutt described a state plan for the improvement of employment services for the Deaf and hard of hearing. This plan was the culmination of two town hall meetings conducted by DVRS and the Deaf community. The presentation was exceptionally well received by those in attendance. I personally would like to thank the New Jersey Association of the Deaf, the Deaf community and DVRS for working collaboratively to develop this new plan. DDHH will work closely as a partner with DVRS in supporting the plan's implementation.

The New Jersey Hearing Aid Project is off to a smooth start. DDHH is responsible for the application process and we have received a large number of inquiries and applications. By the time you receive this edition of the Monthly Communicator the first batch of acceptance letters will have been mailed to eligible applicants. They will then make appointments for a consultation with one of the many licensed audiologists who have agreed to participate in the project. As part of the Project, Montclair State University coordinated a network of audiologists to support this project. They have done an amazing job recruiting a top notch team. For additional information about the New Jersey Hearing Aid Project, please see the article in this edition authored by staff person, Traci Burton.

David C. Alexander, *Ph.D., Director*
New Jersey Division of the Deaf & Hard of Hearing

We Welcome Your Articles and Ads

The Monthly Communicator is published 11 times per year. Deadline for submissions for the March issue is February 1 and should be e-mailed to: *monthlycommunicator@dhs.state.nj.us*.

The deadline for the Monthly Communicator **is the first of the month for the next month.**

Kindly follow these guidelines for submissions:
- Should be less than two pages
- Plain font, such as NY Times #11 or similar
- Type flush left, no tabs
- No art imbedded within
- Send as Word attachment or an e-mail itself
- Art, logos, photos may be sent as attached JPG
- Submissions are not normally repeated
- Content should be of interest to readers, events should be accessible to people with hearing loss, no direct selling products, but educational info about new technology is acceptable
- Editor has discretion regarding editing, without final approval of submitter

Monthly Communicator

State of New Jersey
Department of Human Services
Division of the Deaf and Hard of Hearing

Director: David C. Alexander
Editor: Ira Hock

PO Box 074
Trenton, NJ 08625-0074
Phone: (609) 588-2648 / (800) 792-8339
Videophone: (609) 503-4862
Fax: (609) 588-2528

www.state.nj.us/human services/ddhh

The Monthly Communicator is published by the New Jersey Department of Human Services' Division of the Deaf and Hard of Hearing (DDHH), a state agency. DDHH provides information, referral, and advocacy to service recipients. Information or articles provided by others does not imply endorsement by DDHH or the State of New Jersey. There currently are 8,800 copies of the MC distributed monthly.

I learned how to interact and advocate for people with disabilities through my internships to help the clients find employment or gain services such as Medicare/Medicaid or vocational rehabilitation. These two experiences helped me to visualize how to help the hard of hearing and Deaf populations.

Marc and I had visited a deaf college which opened my eyes to see what Deaf Culture was about. In graduate school, as a class we always went to cultural events to learn or observe American Sign Language. The best way to learn a new language is to immerse oneself.

Reflecting back one day back while I was attending New York University graduate school, the room started to whirl around fifty miles per hour everywhere! Meniere's disease is a "disorder that can cause ringing in the ears, vertigo, hearing loss that has membranous labyrinth (endolymphatic drops) in the ear (VEDA)." This is a sensation of water in the ear that causes imbalance in the inner ear and the person becomes dizzy and nauseous and loss of balance. (VEDA).

I was tested and was diagnosed with Meniere's disease (vertigo) which means that the inner ear has an imbalance and fills up with fluid that can cause dizziness, room spinning, nausea and gait (walking) problems as well as affecting your vision at times. It is best to sit down to try to rest through the attacks and stay calm. This makes take a few hours or a few days to feel better from depending on the individual. Then many years later in graduate school, Meniere's (1999) had progressed after I had a major head on car accident in 1997. At the time I had developed more hearing loss from 42-55 db loss. While I was commuting on a bus and train exacerbated the problem very badly. Also, when I was learning American Sign Language, it had also made me feel worse due to the fast movement. The triggers for me are the following: being near smoking of any kind, strong perfumes or cleaning products, traveling on a plane, train, boat or car, movie theaters or anything in the dark, fast moving objects, flashing lights, stress, supermarkets (stimulus close together), and quick head movements etc. It is very important to keep low stress levels and avoid anything that triggers attacks. Remember everyone is different as well as their reactions to various conditions.

Reflecting back to 9/11/2001 changed the world as we knew it. Breathing in the debris from World Trade Center had caused me to have breathing issues. I lost time from going to school as you could not easily commute from New Jersey to Manhattan. The police made me feel safe when I was commuting during that time.

03/17/2014 10:37

In graduate school we learned about different types of hearing loss and their cultures. I wanted to have valuable information to help myself and others to advocate about hearing loss of all levels and the services that are available. They have state vocational rehabilitation centers to help people pay for college. If you qualify and they have funding available, they may possibly help to pay for hearing aids or FM devices and supported employment or a job coach if needed (all will depend on if they have money in the state you live in and if you financially qualify and you must have a disability.) In colleges they have Special Services to help assist you with services for your disability such as FM devices, permission to tape the class (you will need to talk to your teacher about what you need in the classroom based on your accommodations) or extended time on a test. It is crucial to interact with your doctors to figure out the causation of your hearing loss to make a treatment plan. We learned that hard of hearing people want to hear and can use hearing aids, taking their tests in a quiet place and extra time on a test or quiz if needed (the law states that a person with a disability can have certain accommodations that must match the disability) FM or assistive listening devices, phone amplifiers, television and listening systems, alert systems and public alert systems, CART (which is written words for people to read what is being said in a public place such as a movie theater, closed captioning or note takers. Little d means that you lost your hearing later in life as an adult or child and were hearing most of your life and still want to hear and can use a Cochlear Implant to do so. For example, someone could have Lyme's Disease and lose all of their hearing and obtain a CI, which is done by surgery and remapping the brain to help the individual hear again (not as well but helps to a degree) to function. This population can use an interpreter if they learn American Sign Language but most likely will want a note taker or sit in the front of the classroom/work force.

Lastly, is "D" which is Deaf Culture of when someone is born Deaf and learns American Sign Language to communicate. They will request an interpreter and note takers for services if needed. Animals such as dogs, pigs, gorillas (Koko learned over two hundred words the vocabulary of a two year old child) or dolphins can learn American Sign Language as well. I did teach my dog American Sign Language many years later in time.

It was not easy for me to learn American Sign Language because you need to practice with others when learning a language. I went to many Deaf events and hearing loss events as well to learn the different cultures of hearing loss and to practice American Sign Language. Also, practicing with other students can be helpful as well. You can take tapes out for free in the library (who also has assistive listening devices you can borrow at no cost). I was progressing very well academically then low and behold the problems started. When I signed to people the Meniere's would start. This also occurred while traveling as well by bus and train. I had to stop driving most of the time. I went to Special Services as my hearing was declining and I still had to learn signing. They had suggested a tape recorder as well as an oral interpreter who would help me if I missed a word. I also tried (CART) when someone is typing what the teacher said which I did not like at all. First of all, then you obtain a packet which was fifty pages (this would slow me down) of every little thing someone said which was not always pertinent to the topic. We went back to the drawing board and I asked for a note taker which helped me along with taping the classes which were in voice. Later on, it was much easier. After learning to sign, and then I could watch the interpreter in the classroom if I missed something and also had the teacher to watch, the note taker and an FM system. I was happy when I finally was able to communicate with the Deaf students or teachers there. I learned to ask people to reiterate or write down what they said to help me hear them. This helped with my professionalism and family as well.

An example of this was when Marc and I performed a skit of a married couple of which one spouse had a hearing loss and the other had normal hearing. We showed the public the incorrect way first and then the correct way by Marc coming into the room, tapping me on the shoulder and saying Jen it's time for dinner. There is a lag time for when the hard of hearing or person with hearing loss can hear you because you will have to be made aware of what they said and then understand the speech. The lag for the Deaf would be that the interpreter is always a few minutes behind time of the speaker and then catches the audience up to par.

I had performed two different internships in graduate school for supported employment and vocational rehabilitation. Every state has different names for the vocational rehabilitation or support for hearing loss or other disabilities. (You can google this or look at the state's page where you live.) The services could be for supported employment, job coaches to help the individual on various levels from peace work to regular working on a job. Vocational Rehabilitation was my first internship that I helped people who were mostly hard of hearing. I assisted them in obtaining hearing aids, help with college or services (they would have to first see if they qualify for assistance/make sure the state has money to do that and prove their disability.) I am very fortunate to have a well-rounded cultural experience to have earned my Master's Degree in Education & Deafness Rehabilitation from New York University.

I learned to interact and advocate for people with disabilities through my internships to help clients to find employment or gain services. The second internship was in Brooklyn, NY that I assisted in helping the clients obtain Medicaid or Medicare and various services (these clients mostly were low functioning and performed the same task over and over to earn $1.00 a day). These two experiences were vastly different and helped me to understand the levels of functioning and the need for services.

I will never forget in my undergraduate schooling at Rowan University. There was a student who was blind, who had a perfect GPA but her parents would not allow her to finish school because she was blind. That always made wonder why should she have stopped schooling? I learned about the Blind as well from various students' lectures as well as a worker in the internship at New York University. There was a blind student in my class she was accommodated by using a cane, taping the classes, using an oral method for testing, time and a half for testing, a private location for the testing and using a CCTV (a machine that made the print very large for her to see some of it.) She could have also used a guide dog as well but chose not to do so. (There are trained animals to help with various disabilities.) Also the counselor, who was blind, she was sharper than a whip! She had all of the client's files memorized and helped them very much. Also, there was a student who impressed everyone with her knowledge of Deaf/Blind persons at Helen Keller in Long Island, NY, and showed us tactile signing (signing in your hand.)

It is important to be open minded and show sensitivity to those with disabilities and follow the laws in public places as well as the work force. A hard of hearing person might ask for: assistive listening devices (FM) which brings the sound closer to the hearing aid thru the telephone switch, oral interpreters, or regular interpreter if they know American Sign Language, note takers and sit up front and time and a half on tests if needed. A Deaf person would need an interpreter in the class room, or work force and a note taker as well as flashing lights to alert anyone to a fire in the building. In our classes there were always two interpreters to switch off as they were fatigued quickly.

My thesis consisted of hearing loss, accommodations in the work force or class room and employment of all levels. I researched and had written about how I came to terms with my hearing loss and how it was changing as well as dealing with the Meniere's attacks. I wrote about the different types of hearing loss and accommodations as well as the cultures behind this. For example, my spouse and I visited a college for the Deaf and could see for ourselves how it was all in American Sign Language to communicate with one another. It was history in the making to see it come alive. I was very glad to do this thesis as it helped me advocate for myself as well as others.

The Division for the Deaf and Hard of Hearing is a service that helps this population in New Jersey. They have assistive listening devices in public libraries for people to borrow as well as places to try these devices in the state. They have a "Monthly Communicator" which is a publication for hard of hearing or Deaf events in New Jersey. They also feature Captel which is a phone that has closed captioning that the listener to read what the speaker is saying instead of having to use relay (of going through the operator repeating everything to both parties.

They also show other things that are helpful to a person with hearing loss such as flashing lights to alert you to a doorbell or an alarm. I found this very helpful to look for employment and ways to find groups to practice my American Sign Language and the culture of all forms of hearing loss.

Reflection to the reader—What did I learn about communicating with other people with hearing loss? What is the accommodations for someone on the job or attending classes that has hearing or vision loss? Do you have a disability? How did you advocate for yourself? If you were not successful what did you learn from reading my experiences to help you become a stronger advocate for your job or attending school or seminars?

Once again I had to sit down and think of what to do to finish school in New York. I was somehow able to finish and obtain my Master's Degree through all of those attacks. I also had developed memory problems and was gaining weight rapidly as well as having gait problems (which I did not find out the answers to this many years' later as well as eating and sleeping problems). I also had trouble sleeping for several reasons. I had to sleep with eight pillows to avoid getting dizzy. Also, my spouse snored very loudly and gasped for air. Next, I found him to fall asleep at the wheel while driving and very fatigued after working. We could not figure out what this was all about. I earned my Master's Degree in Deafness Rehabilitation and Education from New York University in 2002. After finishing graduate school, naturally I wanted to find employment and purchase a car. The Meniere's continued and I had serious walking problems and was falling down the stairs in our condo. I had to stop driving, working and was instructed by my doctor to use a cane for my gait.

I also found Shamrock Boutique in Brick, NJ to help with cutting my hair. It is not easy as the vertigo starts with the quick movements. The ladies are very patient with me when that happens.

Reflection: Did you ever have any health setbacks or problems from trying to accomplish your goals? If not what did you do to correct this from happening again in the future?

As for my experiences with audiologists some were beneficial and others were not. Over the years, I had ear infections and burning and itchiness. It turned out that I was allergic to latex that was in the molds of the hearing aids. I found a product called Dry & Store that helped as well to alleviate the problems of ear infections and wax. The product helps by sanitizing hearing aids or cochlear implants as well. It was a number of years before we figured out that this was a huge part of my problem of wearing the hearing aids.

It is important to have classes on how to learn to use the hearing aids or a Cochlear Implant to adjust to one's environment to relearn the sounds (the brain is mapping) this out. The challenges could be locating where the sounds voices are coming from as well as trying to understand what someone is saying. I felt that being proactive is a bonus to wearing my hearing aids! I had a very hard time using the hearing aids and understanding the teachers. The Meniere's as well as feeling of the sweating from the hearing aids caused many problems.

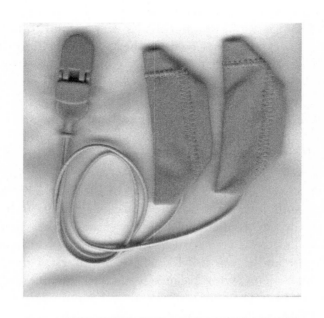

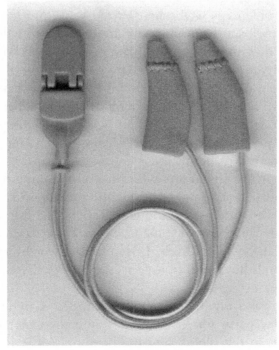

Ear Gear (*www.gearforears*.com, contact Mark Rosal phone number (1-888-766-1838) is also a product that is very helpful to me as well. It is almost like a sock that goes over the hearing aid behind the ear part or a cochlear implant device. You may be wondering how this is helpful to the user? I find that it helps prolong the life of the hearing aid to eliminate the wind, rain, moisture problems and also helps with my psoriasis (anything that touches me where I have psoriasis) can cause a burning or itching problem or if you use any medications for that—this product can help to alleviate the problem. They come in different sizes and colors as well.

In retrospect, we had purchased a car in October 2002 and by the end of the month I was not able to walk once again (I had to have therapy from the car accident in 1997) because of the severity of the Meniere's attacks. It was very hard to function as we had lived in a two floor townhouse and it was not helpful to my illness. I tried Vestibular Therapy (which helps with balance exercises) for the Meniere's. It had caused me high levels of emotional and physical stress. I had the following symptoms: I could not stand, walk or drive, developed eating and memory problems as well when I was twenty nine years old. I had a wealth of knowledge by now about my condition. My hearing loss was also going downhill as well and the memory and Meniere's made graduate school very hard. I worked hard on attending physical therapy for vestibular help with the Meniere's this took many years to maintain. They have many exercises such as using a balance ball, balance exercises such as a beam as well as using a KAT which is a computer that has geometrical shapes to help with the vertigo and balance. You should maintain the exercises at home also.

There were many counselors who misdiagnosed me for many years to say I had bipolar disease (manic highs and lows episodes) which I did not have. I believe that a person should always have a full blood test and a physical before changing any medications. I also started to become allergic to some foods at this time. I tried to lose weight and only could lose several pounds but could not get to the root of the causation of my problems.

One day I was rushed to the hospital in 2004 or 2005 from my husband's holiday party for his job. They informed me that my sugar, triglycerides (fat in the blood) and my hormones were out of control. I was instructed to seek medical help from my doctor immediately and to find an endocrinologist. I did not find that the medical doctors could find the causation of what was happening to my body or develop a proper treatment plan. I did manage to lose about twenty pounds by walking and going to the gym before moving to our new home. They told me that I would have Diabetes within a year if I did not get my weight under control.

We decided to move to find a house without stairs to make it easier for me to function and try to find solutions to our health problems by finding better doctors. I had many baby steps to get back on my feet. I always had a social life and interacted well with others. It is important to me to always build my self-confidence at all times. I feel that it is crucial to have a good support system and doctors to accomplish this. It is also important to believe in yourself in a positive fashion and make short and long term goals. I learned to ask people to repeat themselves or reword what they said. If I still did not grasp the words then I asked them to write it down.

I read an article about Sleep Apnea, a condition that can cause someone to gasp for air and snore so loud you could hear them in another room. I was so glad to find a causation to help Marc as this was very dangerous as he is a meat cutter and as well you need to be fully awake driving a car. We went to a pulmonary doctor who diagnosed him with Sleep Apnea. He was sent overnight to a hospital for a sleep study and it was confirmed. He was fitted with a CPAP that helps him to breathe and night. We were happy to at least find one answer to multiple problems.

A week after moving in to our new home I started to develop new symptoms such as the following: my hair was falling out in clumps, I had difficulty swallowing my food, nails were breaking, I had gained weight had extreme depression, anxiety, more vertigo and fatigue. I immediately hired someone to install grab bars (this helps someone in the bath or shower) you can buy them in a hardware store) this was a preventative so if I did lose my balance in the shower I had something to hold onto. I had told our new doctors of what was occurring at the time and I was not getting anyone to believe me because these symptoms were not reflected in my medical testing as of yet. I finally had an appointment with the new endocrinologist she stated "It sounds like a thyroid issue and hormones as well, we need to run a thyroid ultrasound, new blood work and also place you on medication immediately or you will have Diabetes very soon." I ran the thyroid ultrasound and was pleased to finally have an answer that I had Hypothyroidism which they thyroid controls all of your body and could be solved with hormone replacement. I tried the generic it did not work at all for me. A few months later the thyroid imbalance finally showed up in the blood work. It took me about six months of very hard mood swings to get the proper dose of hormone medication. I was also placed on a diabetes drug to prevent diabetes diagnosis. I also went to a nutritionist to learn how to eat a diabetic diet. My father stated to me "it is time to lose the chains." I did not know what he meant and he wanted me to think differently to be able to pull myself together emotionally and physically. My family was trying to be there for me in the best way they knew how.

To the reader: Did you have an experience of being misdiagnosed or keep having symptoms and not know what to do? It is always important to have a list of symptoms to review with your doctors.

I was finally starting to feel better my hair stopped falling out and my nails stopped breaking etc. Just as I found a good doctor she had to retire because she became ill after her daughter got married. In middle of all of this, I had to find a new doctor to treat me immediately. I did right away and he is still my doctor currently and pleased with the treatment plan. It took over eight years to become diagnosed with Hypothyroidism I was so happy to finally have an answer and find some success with losing about fifty pounds.

03/17/2014 10:40

03/17/2014 10:40

03/17/2014 10:42

Marc and I selected our dog, Lightening, who is a male Shetland Sheepdog so we could have a pet together. I always grew up with Sheltie's in our family, but this was his first pet. He helps with hearing in some ways. He barks to alert me to when a car is coming, or when someone is calling my name; He is sensitive to weather changes. From the barometric pressure you can have Meniere's problems. The one quality that I do love about Lightening is that he "shakes off after something" for example after petting him . . . Maybe I could learn something from that to be able to let things go or shake off my problems. some humor here. Also, when there is a stranger in the street he will bark which is a good thing to protect me from any bad people. We work on agility together (which is a set that I have to help with my balance and to train him as well. The owner trains the dog to weave thru the sticks that you place in the ground. I also trained him to jump on and off a balance board as well for agility. This also helps that I have to walk him all the time which is a bonus to me to keep my weight off.

There is a professional organization, Canine Companions, (*www.cci. org*) that trains dogs to assist people with various disabilities. The dog could assist the person crossing the street, alerting someone if their sugar is too low or if they are going to have a seizure. The dog acts as a companion as well as a service dog that has as license from special training and you must carry that with you in the store or wherever you bring your dog. The dog can also assist the individual on the job as well to open doors and alert the individual to any dangers they may encounter. This also helps with self-esteem and forms a loving bond between the dog and the owner.

A few months later in 2005, I developed headaches once again and still had a very hard time losing weight and eating my food without having problems. We found a vitamin (B Complex that helps with tinnitus and Meniere's) that helped me tremendously. Also, my new medical doctor had suggested physical therapy for the headaches and other injuries. In the past, the physical therapists did not have vestibular training and when working on my neck or back it would set that off. We addressed the problem together to find a therapist who encompassed the knowledge of all three problems. She used a KAT (which is a computer idea with the screen consisting of geometrical and moving shapes and moving your feet at the same time to help with the balance. She also had me use a balance beam and various exercises on a balance ball (that I could replicate at home). If you only go to therapy and do not practice the exercises at home you are defeating your purpose. I finally started to see some positive results with my gait and headaches. I was starting to walk for five minutes and keep improving my time without falling down with using the cane that I was prescribed. It was not easy at all. Sometimes there are flare-ups and if you perform the home exercises or go back to the therapist for a short time you can get better again. She also had dogs with her to motivate the patients as well. I had reflected back upon my grandpa's statements that "knowledge is power" to be able to get through the hard times. It is very important to have emotional support when dealing with life events to help you "believe in yourself. I had to make several lifestyle and dietary changes once again. My parents presented several articles to me about Celiac Disease. Celiac Disease is "an autoimmune disease that is triggered by gluten found in wheat barley and rye." It can cause rashes and attack the small intestines as well and have constipation. The only cure is to avoid gluten which can be found in food, medicines or makeup etc."(Celiac disease.net.) I went to a Gastronologist in my new town to try to find an answer of what was causing me to have issues with this area. I was instructed to keep a diary of what I was eating and symptoms afterward. He diagnosed me with Celiac Disease (which turned out to be a gluten allergy one of the many allergens found in food and medication) as well as sending me to an allergist. I was happy to find an answer to my problem and asked the health food stores to help me to eliminate gluten from my diet.

However; the allergist stated that I am allergic to all the main allergens: nuts, eggs, soy, wheat, gluten, dairy, fish and shellfish. It is now required by law to list allergens on food drinks, health and beauty aids and some medications as well have them listed. This was not always the case and was hard to figure this out. Also, the people who are affected with allergies should use separate utensils and cooking in different pans to be safe from allergens. If you go out to eat or go to your doctors you should tell them what you are allergic to. My medical doctor sent me to a nutritionist to help me plan an allergy free diet in addition to the diabetic diet and to lose weight. Now, I had an even larger job to start all over again, the health food store owners and staff was so helpful to me. I also learned that I could not take medications as well because I am allergic to them. Even though, I was eating so healthy I did not know that I was allergic to all of the food I was consuming and once again happy to have found some intestinal and migraine relief. I had to learn to space out my meals, eating every two to three hours, cut out caffeine and lower my sugar (by monitoring it with a glucose monitor) etc. I was finally able to start walking more and after obtaining the proper diagnosis and taking the correct medications and diet I was finally able to lose fifty pounds at this point. It was not an easy feat as you can see. I would say that the secret to my success of losing weight and keeping it off is to weigh and measure all of your food and exercise at least thirty minutes a day.

Nature's Nutrition in Brick, NJ, is always very helpful to me. The owner, Peter Marino, is a pharmacist as well. The staff is always helpful as well with any questions that I have about nutrition or health. The contact information is (732)920-3637 or *www.naturesnutritionstores.com* on 383 Brick Blvd, Brick, New Jersey 08723. They can order you food by the case to save money on some items and always have a discount to help you pay for the food. They have the following types of products: fruits and vegetables, organic, allergy free foods, gluten, wheat, dairy, fish, nuts etc. as well as vegetarian or vegan foods as well. A vegetarian is someone who may or may not eat fish or dairy. A vegan eats all natural products that are not from an animal or its products. My brother is a vegan and eats healthy. I always accommodate him when he comes over for a visit with pasta and salad which makes him happy! The store also has health information on their website if you need more information.

It took me over eight years to find out what the problems were and how to find solutions were not easy. I also have PCOS which is irregular periods and cysts painful on the ovaries. The Metformin is supposed to help to control this as well. After going to Pete Marino with all of my medical conditions we sat down and tried to figure out which foods I could eat that did not have allergies in them. We figured out that I could eat organic white part of the egg not the yellow, organic apples, and certain cookies that does not have any allergens in them as well as ice cream that are made from rice. I brought all of the food labels to the nutritionist to make a game plan on how to eat all over again. At that point I had sixty eight pounds off in about three years. I went from a size twenty four to a twelve! I did lose eighty eight pounds altogether and went to a size ten and had to gain some of it back as I became too thin at one point and it caused me to have more health problems.

03/17/2014 10:38

My brother stated the following: "Vegetarians eat dairy as well as fruits and vegetables. It is believed that some also eat fish or chicken. Vegans, on the other hand, consume no animal products or by-products, which include milk, fish, chicken, meat or honey. People who are vegan receive the same benefits that non-vegans do, but without animal cruelty. All of their nutrients come from plants: fruits, vegetables, nuts, seeds, lentils, tofu, soy, seitan, etc. Vegans follow the path for many reasons, which may include some combination of animal rights, the environment, health, and fitness. The vegan lifestyle is not a diet, nor is it a fad. It is catching on with leaps and bounds, and even many celebrities are following a vegan diet such as former President Bill Clinton, Al Gore, former boxer, Mike Tyson, actor/actress, Toby Maguire/Natalie Portman, baseball player, Prince Fielder and even Oprah Winfrey had three hundred and seventy eight of her staff to have a vegan diet for one week and for some it make a permanent change."

To the reader—Did you ever have a health problem or series of problems and did not know the causation or what to do about them? It is important to have a list of your medications and all of your symptoms to explain to your doctor. Sometimes it is also ok if you bring another person with you to assist you with the process. HLAA has stickers that are put on a person's chart who has hearing loss as well as a packet for hearing loss if you need to be hospitalized as well.

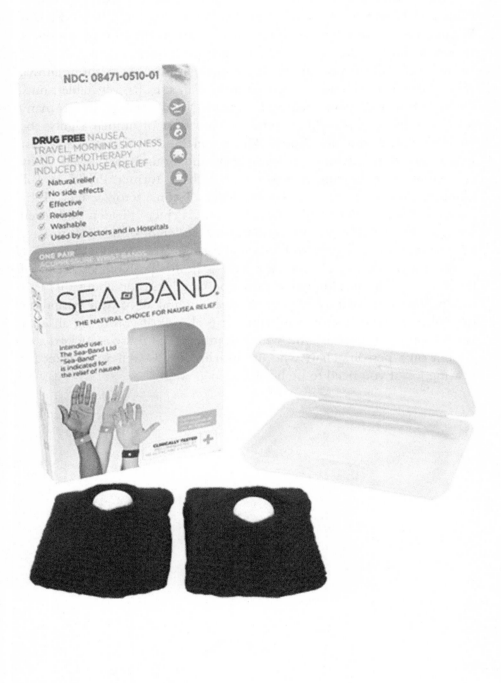

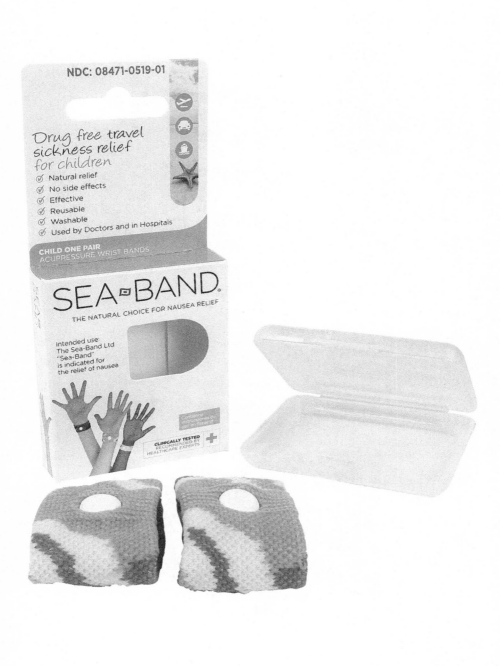

NDC: 08471-0547-01

24 PIECES – WEIGHT: 1.35G EACH

GINGER
GUM

SEA=BAND.

ANTI-NAUSEA
GINGER
GUM

FOR TRAVEL, MORNING SICKNESS
AND CHEMOTHERAPY INDUCED
NAUSEA RELIEF

☑ Safe, all natural relief of nausea
☑ Gluten free

THE NATURAL CHOICE
ANTI-NAUSEA GINGER GUM

SEA◦BAND.

THE NATURAL CHOICE FOR NAUSEA RELIEF

I wanted to find something to help me sit in the car to prevent motion sickness and previously I had tried a relief band that tore off skin to help with motion sickness that was not efficient and very expensive. Later on, I also found that using a Sea—Band (there are pulse points) to wear something to help with the vertigo on your wrist (this can be worn for motion sickness, Chemotherapy or pregnancy etc.) that helped me sit in the car, return to work later on in time. They also sell other products such as ginger gum that can help with nausea as well. Their information is *www.sea-band.com* and sell other natural products as well.

I found a Dry and Store product *www.dryandstore.com* that is also very helpful to me. It is almost like using a nail dryer idea. You are using an Ultraviolet light that sanitizes the hearing aids or cochlear implants. It helps with preventing wax buildup and ear infections. You can find their information on www.dryandstore.com.

My husband is a very patient and loving man with everything. We went to counseling together to try to learn how to cope with our health problems. Marc and I bought cell phones that have a microphone and is hearing aid compatible to help me hear on the cell phone. We had a new theory at the time that the Meniere's could be triggered from wearing bifocal glasses (looking up and down) could cause that to happen or from diet or other theories?

One day the doctor advised that I should use a cane. I was very depressed and did not interact with anyone except my husband and with my family. I could not believe this from a healthy woman and right after finishing such a challenging graduate program. Little by little, I started to improve. After accepting that the Meniere's was at its worst ever from the sensation of tables jumping and rooms spinning and being ill after eating a healthy diet I wanted to seek further help for my conditions which were unknown to me at the time.

I believe that talking things through is crucial and having a positive outlook and sharing with a support system is relevant to one's success. After a year of Vestibular physical therapy, I have started to see some success and maintained the home exercises. I also mentioned this to my mom and aunt who saw a commercial about a vitamin B that helps with Vertigo as well as tinnitus (which is a loud ringing or roaring in one's ears—sensation of this from medication, hearing loss or other problems. It is really up to the individual to be proactive about their health to obtain the correct treatment and follow through. Overall, when you diagnosed it is up to you to gather the research and present your symptoms to your doctor. I always advise to write it down to have questions ahead of time prepared. This will quell anxiety of forgetting to ask a question. You can always call your health plan's nurse to gather information or a local library or computer. I have applied my learning and dedication that I learned from my education to cope with the health conditions. However, I felt in time that I still had plenty of the health symptoms but with the proper support, nutrition and exercise I can lessen the severity of the problems.

Reflection: Did you ever have a health problem that you did not know what the causation was that lingered for years? It is important to have a list of symptoms to bring the doctor and also to talk to the nurses as well.

Right after trying to heal myself we learned that my grandma was very ill with cancer. She was most loved by everyone who knew her because she gave of herself. She was very skilled in ceramics, painting, and dancing. We had reminisced as a family how important my grandpa was as well to us. I had to stop wearing the hearing aids for a short time to feel better from the attacks. My grandma always said "there is light at the end of the tunnel." My grandfather always said "knowledge is power." It is always crucial to stop and think before acting and learning about new things in your life. However; believing in oneself is half the battle.

Reflection to the reader: This story is meant to be uplifting to the reader. I am now having a stronger and more positive outlook and wonderful support system. Illness is always a difficult thing and affects the whole family. However; you will not lose your sense of being and the power of believing that you can feel better in life. There is always hope to get better from the situations we are in. I also use a time of reflection and write things out that I want to track every so often be it finances, my life or how I had handled something before and how would I handle it again? Have you ever tried to journalize or use free association? Free association is writing about a topic or a word not worrying about sentence format or spelling. Writing has always been an outlet for me to get my thoughts together and making a plan of action for situations in my life. Also, exercising, meditating or other hobbies can be an outlet as well. I had slowly improved by walking to the mailbox, then five minutes and built upon this every day to work on my balance issues. Eventually you will see success or light at the end of the tunnel. For example, after losing five pounds you will feel better.

Have you ever been in a situation that you thought would never subside? How did you handle it?

In 2007, we lost my grandmother (on my mom's side) to ovarian and stomach cancer which was very traumatic for my family. She was a ray of sunshine in everything in our lives from graduation to my marriage. She always said: "There is light at the end of the tunnel." Grandma was very active in her ceramics, painting and had many friends. We had other challenges in that year as well.

Marc had lazy eye growing up and it had progressed into double vision and required major invasive eye surgery. It was a very difficult time period in our lives, with grandma being ill from cancer and the shingles. My father had prostate cancer two times and also survived the attacks on both World Trade Center events. I will never forget the kindness of my brother's girlfriend at the time: She took us for Marc's eye surgery and as soon as he was released from that we were summoned to grandma's last moments in the same day! I had reacted by whole body developed psoriasis for the first time shortly after. It is very true, that you cannot understand something unless you live in someone else's shoes. I truly understand the suffering that my grandma endured with the psoriasis. Somehow, I had started to become stronger emotionally in 2006 and 2007 from my own medical problems. My parents and grandparents always instilled inner strength in my brother and I growing up.

Soon after this devastating loss, I was able to return to work after five long years of my health conditions and family duress. I was hired to teach psychology as an adjunct in a community college. Later in time, I also worked in other areas of the college such as: developmentally delayed adults, honor students, tutoring and administration. I taught the developmentally delayed adults, Life Skills Classes, such as: Laughter is the Best Medicine I and II, Time and Money Management and Bullying. I was able to assist people who had strokes, Down Syndrome or other problems. It was not easy to communicate with this group and it was challenging for me. I taught honors psychology and enjoyed that very much as they motivated themselves. I tutored students with disabilities on campus when needed. Part of my job was to be a liaison to the school working off campus at night to ensure safety, rules and regulations, and assist the teachers.

I had another challenge to overcome with dry eye syndrome. Symptoms can occur whenever there is someone smoking, dust, florescent lighting, heavy close eye or computer work it would flare up. My ophthalmologist fitted me with punctual plugs that are inserted in your tear ducts to help with the burning and itchiness in my eyes. He also prescribed Refresh and Restatis. Later in time, he assisted me with a gel mask that heats up in the microwave and punctual plugs in the upper lids. This protocol helped me to have some relief from the problem.

I enjoyed working as an adjunct of Psychology and used message boards and email to communicate outside of the classroom. I used my FM and hearing aids as well as informing the students that I am hard of hearing. The students enjoyed performing skits of various disabilities and accommodations that went hand in hand. Through my perseverance, I wore a button that said, "Please face me so I can read your lips", which was a constant reminder for the students to help me if I missed a word. They also helped my raising their hand so I could figure out who was speaking. There is a delay in hearing someone when you have hearing loss you must first figure out where the sound or speakers are and then try to figure out what they are saying. The staff repeated themselves or wrote things down to assist me. They used a microphone in the meetings most of the time. One year a classroom was very loud from machinery. I requested a different room and was accommodated. I also used the FM to help me hear on my cell phone which has a Blue tooth capability. It also assisted me with taking classes online to hear the speakers.

I divided the class into several small groups and taught them life experiences of how to advocate for disabilities. We had many skits and scenarios of the child study team and work place as well. I assigned the disabilities to be hearing and vision loss as they are the most common and they had to present it to the class on how they would help the child (by assuming the roles of parents, educators, doctors and the students with a disability.) It is so important to make sure that you ask nicely and make sure that the disability matches the accommodations you are seeking. I find it crucial to see the person first not the disability. For example, if the person has a hearing loss and is a student they can ask for the following accommodations: sitting in the front, time and a half on tests or projects, to tape the class, use an FM, have an interpreter if need be, for the teacher to reiterate what the students said if needed. For vision loss a proper accommodation could be: sitting in the front, taping the class, having the tests orally administered or using large print on a CCTV, a cane or a guide dog if needed. When the child is attending kindergarten through high school, the parent will advocate for their needs. In college, the student must learn to ask for accommodations by themselves to the Special Services Departments or later on in life to their jobs.

I had another challenge of having excessive dry eye symptoms. They can be caused by florescent lights or lights flickering, smoking or strong smells, close eye work, the glare from our computers or phones. My ophthalmologist fitted me with punctual plugs to help me see as well as eye drops. Later in time, he assisted me with a gel heating pack to help with the dry eye symptoms.

To the reader: What did you learn about communicating with someone who has vision or hearing loss? What are the levels of hearing loss and support groups? What accommodations might one expect in the classroom for individuals who have hearing or vision loss as a student or on the job? Where you ever denied accommodations and what did you do about this to turn it around? Did you have a smooth process in advocating for yourself or your child?

To the reader: Has anyone ever treated you wrongly? Name at least two ways. How would you correct the situation?

In retrospect, I was diagnosed with PCOS (Polycystic Ovarian Syndrome which the patient develops cysts on her ovaries and can cause infertility) and we never dreamed that we would face infertility. I was so ashamed and cried about this with my spouse. It was not fair people around me were able to plan their pregnancies and here we were unable to conceive. Marc and I tried to make a game plan after several years of trying to have a baby. Even after being placed on Metformin, a drug that could help regulate my periods, there was no success. Even after losing the weight it did not make a difference.

Marc and I decided to try private adoption. We had tried for over five years to adopt privately and did not succeed. The birthmothers ran away with our money or decided to use multiple drugs to make the babies very sick. We were thinking what else could we do? We lost a life's fortune and I became very depressed once again from this failure. We looked into surrogacy and IVF In-Vitro Fertilization treatments. They were very expensive and our insurance only covered the testing to find out why we could not conceive. We also found out we both had issues in this department. Our next step was trying foster or adoption care through the state. We soon learned that we did not have the training (background of working with very severe cases in our lives: such as Autism, Down Syndrome, physical and mental disabilities.) We tried foster care and decided that was not for us either. The goal is to reunify the child and their families some of the children are abused in mental or physical fashions. The family has one year or so to get help so that they can reunify with their child hopefully. In all the adoption or foster care facilities you must take pass the requirements for a home study (which varies from agency to agency and the age of the children you are willing to care for) parenting classes, obtain fingerprinting to make sure you are not a criminal and have a good job to ensure you obtain a license to have a child through the state or private adoption. We did not succeed at our goal and currently taking a time out (2014) as you will see later in the story.

Reflection: Have you had a medical issue that prevented you from the becoming pregnant or to take care of other people be it your family member or otherwise? What did you do to obtain help for your situation?

In 2008, just a short time after losing grandma and getting back on my feet, my father was diagnosed with Leukemia which is a deadly cancer. His brother was also diagnosed with that as well and died very quickly as he did not want to endure much of a treatment plan. I was able to tell my dad about some of my promotions. My father suffered for two full horrible years of treatment of chemotherapy and radiation that did not work. The hospital administered R—CHOP (Retuxin) which is the strongest type of chemotherapy. They gave him morphine to try to help with the pain he was in that was caused by the cancer. One of the drugs had affected his vision at times. My father was a college graduate and worked for thirty seven years for the telephone company and it was disheartening to see him undergo losing his intelligence from the cancer and its treatments.

On the first day of the January 2010 semester, my mom called us to report to the hospital immediately to say goodbye to our loving father. I had to call out from work for one week and Marc only was allowed three days to be absent. I found that it was extremely difficult to teach in front of a classroom while I was in mourning. We were in total shock as a family and could not believe that we lost grandma and dad in such a short time period. I learned very quickly who my friends were. Some of the "so called" friends told me off because I didn't listen to them after two hours of listening to their problems during the time I was in mourning. I thought that they would be there to help us through the grief.

Yet, here were many kind people who did listen and help support us, be it a phone call, visit, card etc. It is always up to the family to try to heal together. Some of the ways that helped us to heal are: grief counseling, journalization, exercising, meditating or bereavement meetings.

That semester was extremely difficult for the students who cried to me about their problems as well. One female student confided in me about domestic violence, I had to instruct another student to please have the others read the book quietly, while I attended to this. I referred her to counseling and used my follow up skills to make sure she was away from the abuser. I was able to help other students as well with their hardships.

Somehow we moved on as a family and are still trying to grow individually and together. I find that it is crucial to always have the strong bond with my mom, my brother and Marc that no one could ever break no matter how hard they might try. I still would like to see more for my family to heal and not be sad to have enjoyed our grandparents and my father in our lives. I went to therapy faithfully and still go for grief counseling. They do have bereavement groups and moving on groups for people who lose a family member and need assistance with this.

Just as life was settling down, Marc started to have a myriad of health problems once again. His symptoms were: running to the bathroom, drinking an excessive amount of water and had extreme fatigue (he would fall asleep.) We thought that he was getting diabetes as it runs in his family. After going to the main doctor we were referred to a nephrologist (kidney specialist.) We learned that he had inherited a kidney problem that did not break down the protein in the urine, that was confirmed via biopsy, blood and urine tests. Kidney patients are required to have twenty four hour urine tests to make sure the medicaitons are working. The medications had side effects that can change one's moods and energy levels. It is crucial for the patient to notice any changes and report them to your doctor immediately from a new or old medication. We felt the pills were helpful as they lowered the protein in the urine count from Presidone but also made him gain weight as well. We noticed that he was not getting better and the doctor referred him to another specialist in New York who placed him on stronger medication. We wanted to try this but after a short while of being on the new medication it had more side effects that he had several falls and was treated in the ER. It also affected his wellbeing and memory. He was then placed back onto a milder drug which is helping him much better with the protein problem and lost about twenty pounds. (He had gained over seventy five to a hundred pounds in a short time which was very scary for us.)

Reflection to the reader—Did you ever have a side effect from medication or a series of symptoms that might be a different disease then you thought it might be? How did you go about solving it? What were the results? Did you maintain the problem as best as you can? What can you do differently the next time something happens to you or someone else to present the symptoms to a doctor?

In 2012, I answered my cell phone and it was not Marc on his cell phone and I started to feel anxiety. A lady from his job called to inform me that Marc was taken to the Emergency Room for dismembering (cutting off) two of his fingers from using a band saw (He is a meat cutter by trade.) The doctor was wonderful and was able to reattach his fingers. This accident on the job was a very traumatic experience both emotionally and physically. He developed nightmares for about a year and cried all the time. (He was such a brave person before the kidney diagnosis and this problem.) I had to hire a home health aide to assist him with bathing, cutting his food or anything he might need. He was more than double my weight and it was impossible to move him by myself.

He had to go on Workman's Compensation for several months. They had covered the costs of medical services such as: for transportation everywhere as he was not allowed to drive, occupational therapy and a home health aide. I was working at the college and the purpose of having the home health aide would be to monitor him when I was not home or when he needed more assistance. Finally, he was cleared to drive again, but still could not dress, shower or cook for himself as of yet. He started to take me to my job. I had expected the aide to have him showered and cook his food for him and have Marc be ready to take me to work. The man was very lazy and I fired him because he was causing fires on my stove and just sitting there and not assisting him. Somehow, I was able to try to take over once again to shower, dress him and help him with his food etc. It took him over a year to regain strength (not all of it) but returned to the job after only three and a half months.

I used my inner strength to help me and asked people who were close to me for assistance if I needed. My mom and brother were very helpful with household chores or taking us to the doctors if needed or a ride for me to work (cabs are very expensive.) I did give the in-laws a few chores to assist as well. I found that the emotional support was very crucial to help us get through this time period.

Shortly after, he started he winced in pain from his shoulder (probably from years of repetitive lifting heavy things and working in the meat room) and required surgery in 2013. The pain started around October 2013. It wasn't even a few months after his finger issue to have more to deal with. We had tried one doctor that my gut feeling was that he couldn't even read the MRI correctly to us.

Also, the physical therapy he wanted to send us to was out of network as well and wanted an exorbitant amount. In the middle of the treatment and after booking the surgery I called and cancelled everything. We searched for another orthopedic surgeon. We found one that was referred to us via a professional that we knew.

Reflection to the reader: Did you ever go to a doctor and not feel confident in their services? What did you do to modify the situation? How would you handle this in the future if your instincts tell you that this is not the right doctor or situation for you?

He was wonderful and explained the MRI in detail and what the surgery involved the recovery process as well. We decided that this was a much better game plan and felt confident to book the surgery with the orthopedic surgeon. It is so important to feel confident in the doctor and treatment plan!

We were very pleased with the surgeon that had performed ten different surgeries to his shoulder and that the surgery was successful. Now, having some experience with caring for people, this was slightly easier for me to approach. He had to go through physical therapy once again. Emotionally, it was difficult for him as he was not allowed to do anything except watch television or read a magazine for two months. He also gained back all of his weight he lost from last year and more. We were scared about that but knew from experience that he would go back to the gym and lose the weight again. We worked as a team, he would tell me what he needed at least most of the time and if not then I tried to guess what type of help he would need. (I found it very hard both times through the surgery for him to tell me what he needed me to do.) Here I was emotionally and physically exhausted from everything going to work and caring for people for so many years.

I am very grateful for my inner strength once again that helped me get through this. My mom stated "Prioritize your goals." I found that difficult but if a chore had to wait then it would have to wait because I was being stretched very thin energy wise (as my conditions do flare up when exhausted or overstimulated.) My mom will always be "my rock" as my support system. She came down to help when she could. My brother also tried to cheer us on. My in-laws tried to give emotional support. Again, I saw which people cared and who did not during all of this. My friend and her spouse volunteered to help us for a weekend of helping me clean the house which I am very grateful for. I am also grateful for the professionals who listened to us during our times of need. He was finally cleared medically to return to work in the summer of 2013. I was tested to see if I was low on any vitamins and found out that I was low in Vitamin D and Calcium. Once I was on the correct vitamins then most of the psoriasis went away (I still have to use medication from the dermatologist as well). I also believe that as I was getting stronger mentally from all of this as well and trying to manage my stress better.

Time for reflection: Do you have a good support system? What does the term friend or family member mean to you? If you do not have a support system what will you do to obtain one? Did you have success after dealing with a medical or work situation?

I also started Jenny's Tutoring to tutor in the following: Psychology, Special Needs, and English as a Second Language, basic American Sign Language, resume help, and finding a job from ages five and up. I also obtained a promotion to administrator at the college. In 2012, my hearing changed again from forty two-seventy decibels loss. I had a very hard time understanding speech for the first time in my life on the radio, television and when people were talking. I was fitted with stronger hearing aids and an FM to assist me on the job. The Meniere's and Thyroid attacks caused my hearing to fluctuate (it varies from person to person some can lose all of their hearing or some of it from Meniere's attacks.) If they lose all of their hearing they can be fitted with a Cochlear Implant or communicate with American Sign Language. I was still doing very well with the hearing aids and FM in the work force.

Then, low and behold, in January 2013, I was informed that I would not have my positions at the college. The off campus location for the administrator only wanted to have their staff to be in charge because of the shootings in the schools. Also, I qualified for a raise as an adjunct which I did obtain, only to learn that the Middle States required your Master's Degree to be in the subject matter you are teaching. I was given the raise and then let go. I was devastated after working so hard to get on my feet and then to fall flat!

Time for reflection: Did you ever lose your job or in that situation now? What can you differently about the situation? Where you ever in a situation that was complicated and you solved it? How can you resolve it easier next time?

My substitute teaching licensure was still open so I tried that once again. There were too many physical barriers for me to succeed at this such as not always having an elevator. Then I realized that I could not physically perform that job. It is now nine months since I lost my job and it is quite difficult emotionally, physically and financially. Then in December of 2013 the state of New Jersey ran out of money to assist people with unemployment who were on it for so long. The new trend it that people are living on their retirement funds, declaring bankruptcy or foreclosure when they cannot claim unemployment as there are very few jobs in this state.

At first, I was very upset about the losing of my job, but am able to start healing in some ways. I feel that pursuing Reiki (healing energy and meditation) was helpful to learn how to meditate and opened my mind to other areas. By taking a class it helped me to realize that I do have the strength to finish writing this book and having It published to help other people. I have been writing this book for seven years and decided that this is the time I can use effectively to heal and publish my book. I am hoping that good things will start to happen financially with a good job and feel better emotionally from all of this. We are experiencing severe financial hardships, mental and physical problems that I am diligently working on through writing, journalizing, spending time with my family and friends. I always reflect a few ways to think of who I can work through stressful situations. Also, role playing the situations out in advance can be helpful as well.

What do you do to distress and regroup? I enjoy using coupons in the supermarkets to save over fifty to one hundred dollars every week. Sometimes all you need to do is tweak your approach and change will come your way. It is important to have a good support system of family, friends and doctors to help you get through life. Always look at a situation and try to find the positive ray of hope in the rainbow! I feel that if you work very hard to pursue your dreams they will happen someday. We all have challenges in our lives that make us stronger. I have finally accepted my hearing loss and other disabilities that I do have. I will continue to persevere and find employment. After eight struggling years I finally achieved my success of researching, editing and writing, "Hear" I am!! I am very proud of myself for finishing this book and it was very therapeutic to write this for me! Always be willing to tweak things or have a different perspective on things. Remember you can also choose to embark on a journey in your life as well! Thank you very much for reading my story and developing the power and knowledge inside yourself to succeed!

03/17/2014 10:43

WORKS CITED

ALDA-GS. Association for Late Deafened Adults. Organization for hearing loss. Page 7, 20

APO, Alpha Phi Omega. National Coed Service Fraternity. Rowan University, 1995-1996: Page 15,16

Beilis, Jennifer. Author. *"Hear" I am!!* 2006-2014.

Beilis, Marc. Spouse. 1998: Page 6.

Brookdale Community College, Lincroft, New Jersey. 1991-1994: Page 9, 12

Canine Companions for Independence. *www.cci.org*. National Organization that trains dogs for people with disabilities: Page 41. *www.celiacdisease.net Page 42*

Division of the Deaf and Hard of Hearing and "The Monthly Communicator" helps people with hearing loss: Page 32

Dry and Store, *www.dryandstore.com*, helps people clean their hearing aids and cochlear implants. Page 27.

Ear Gears. Rosal, Marc. *www.gearforears.com* Page 36, 18 *www.everydayhealthmedia.com* Page 9

G. C., mentor in hearing loss, NJ 1998—current. Page 6-8.

HLAA, Hearing Loss Association for America. *www.hearing* loss.org, Page 18-19

Nature's Nutrition, Marino, Peter. *www.naturesnutrition.com* page 43 and website www.naturesnutritionstores.com

New York University, New York, thesis, 1999–2002. Page 24–32

Pictures credit to Chris Nichols

Rowan University, Glassboro, NJ. 1994–1996: Page 15–16, 32

Sea-Band products *www.sea-band.com*. Page 49

Shamrock Boutique, hair and nails, Brick, NJ. Page 34

VEDA Vestibular Disorders articles. Page 11.

Testimonials

Jenny has successfully made inroads in educating the public about the impact of what is an invisible disability of hearing loss on individuals. C.G. in New Jersey

Jenny Beilis has written a powerful book that finds its strength in the perseverance and optimism she has exhibited throughout her long-term battle with hearing loss, disability and illness. In the face of great challenges that would defeat even the strongest and healthiest of people, Jenny has found ways to repeatedly survive, redirect her life and flourish. Her book is full of information and personal wisdom to help others. Reflective questions thoughtfully interspersed (placed) throughout the text helps readers sort through their own issues and find inner strength. Jenny's can do attitude and giving nature prevail with inspiration and empowerment even amid descriptions of the hardest of times. We can all learn coping mechanisms from her endurance, positive outlook, and devotion to making a difference. Jenny's book is universally valuable for all people, especially those seeking hope and encouragement in the face of hearing loss and illness. It is also an enriching read for anyone who wishes to increase their awareness of disability rights and issues.

L.H., New Jersey educator, late deafened adult and advocate for people with hearing loss

A very creative, interactive self-help book, with suggestions and teachings coming from an experienced writer, who advocates for people with disabilities!

Highly Recommended!

T.J. Educator, Hospital worker in New Jersey

"Hear" I am!! serves as an inspiration and provides hope to anyone struggling with a physical or emotional dilemma. Jennifer's tenacity to set goals and turn dreams into reality is highly motivating. After reading this book you leave with a positive reason to wake up and welcome your tomorrow. I loved it and look forward to a sequel.

S.R.S., New Jersey educator, Master's degree

COMMENTS

Jen I am so proud of you for writing your book *"Hear" I am!!*. Keep it up and I know you will be successful with your future stories! Marc and my brother stated that they are both very proud of my accomplishments physically and emotionally!

My aunt Fran stated that she is very proud of me by overcoming my problems and obtaining my goals to help others.

One mother of a student I had who has Down Syndrome exclaimed: "Thank you so much for helping my son to make sentences when speaking and reading. I never thought that would be possible!"

From other students over the years: "I am so grateful that Mrs. Beilis was able to help me advocate for my needs in the classroom."

Another student's parent informed me that their son who has developmentally delays was able to volunteer in a church and to start dating. She was so happy that I taught him valuable life skills that transferred from the classroom to real life!

One student had Traumatic Brain Injury and cannot talk, think correctly (a stroke affected the Weinereke's and Broca's area) or write. The caregiver was so grateful that I helped him to find other ways to express himself through my being patient with him to interact with the other student's learning Life Skills!

Thank you for teaching my daughter English as a Second Language. The student was able to learn her alphabet, numbers . . . and now does very well in school!

You are such an inspiration to me! From a friend who has multiple disabilities

Made in the USA
Las Vegas, NV
15 August 2021